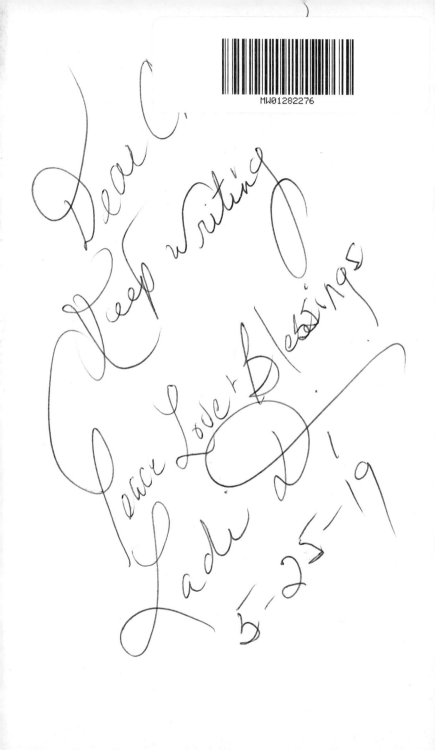

Dear C.

Keep writing

Peace Love + Blessings

Ladi D
5-25-19

Forever In Your Eyes

poems

SYLVIA DIANNE BEVERLY

authorHOUSE®

AuthorHouse™
1663 Liberty Drive
Bloomington, IN 47403
www.authorhouse.com
Phone: 1 (800) 839-8640

Published by AuthorHouse 11/02/2018

ISBN: 978-1-5462-6671-6 (sc)
ISBN: 978-1-5462-6670-9 (e)

Print information available on the last page.

Any people depicted in stock imagery provided by Getty Images are models,
and such images are being used for illustrative purposes only.
Certain stock imagery © Getty Images.

This book is printed on acid-free paper.

Because of the dynamic nature of the Internet, any web addresses or links contained in this book may have changed since publication and may no longer be valid. The views expressed in this work are solely those of the author and do not necessarily reflect the views of the publisher, and the publisher hereby disclaims any responsibility for them.

Dedicated to Dr. Maya Angelou,
a.k.a. Marguerite Johnson,
for her generosity in sharing greatly with many,
her writings, especially her poetry.
"You've inspired me for decades
and I appreciate your work 'phenomenally'!"

Acknowledgements

All praises to God first and foremost. I thank God for giving me creative talents and for blessing me perpetually, enabling me to share with others. All that I do is prayerfully, by the grace of God.

A very special "thank you" to my mother, Dorothy E. Beverly, my #One Fan, for her love and encouragement, who instilled in me and my eight brothers and sisters, that with prayer all things are possible. "Mom, your support is phenomenal."

I thank my dad, the late Daniel Levi Beverly, Sr., for his generous devotion of love, pride, wit, sharing, caring and strong support. "I miss our daily association, I'll always be 'Daddy's Girl'."

Many thanks to my brothers the late Daniel Levi, Jr., Anthony DeWitt, and the late David "Dawud" Beverly for their charm, gentlemen ways, love and appreciation.

Many more thanks to my sisters, the late Bernadette Shafer, Linda, Karen and Donna Beverly, for their love, beauty, support and strength (you'll always be my babies). Thank you tenderly to my youngest sibling, my baby, Kimberly Teresa Beverly, who has consistently encouraged me with love, support and insistence.

Thanks to my special sister, my friend, my partner,

Cynthia Brawner-Jackson for her love and encouragement and for sharing life in abundance.

To my Godmother, the late Ethel B. Dorsey, thanks to her for expressing that she could foresee this publication, along with others and for her love and prayers. Thank you to my Godparents, the late Joseph Albert and Mary Azalia Brawner for their love and encouragement.

Thanks to my sister Jamila Beverly Akil-Robichaux for her recognition of my creative abilities, early on and her unconditional love.

Thank you to my uncle, my friend, Clarence Eltra Beverly, Jr., who I've shared a special relationship since childhood, "your love is King."

With perpetual gratitude and appreciation, thank you to Franklin Sonn, former South African Ambassador to the United States of America for the gracious words stated in the FOREWORD of this book. "I'm encouraged."

Thank you to my Special Aunt Dutch, for your love, inspiration, friendship and daily prayers.

Here's to my sisterhood of poets, "Collective Voices", the late Margie Jones, Angela Turnbull, Joy Alford, Billye Keene-O'Kera and Carolyn Cooley-Joyner the journey has been great, stay on a daily mission and smile with reflections of LOVE.

Thanks to my mentees and special friends Kisha Morris and LaTashia Middleton, our relationship has blossomed like gorgeous butterflies, golden sunshine and precious jewels-you inspire me greatly.

My youth poetry group "Girls and Boys With Hearts", Bernadette Brown, Jessica Gaines, Rochqual Cain, Dana Makel, Nina Makel, Asantewa Disroe, Myisha Robinson,

Daquane Robinson, Kyndall Brown, Monique Brown, Alonna Hagans, Ada Mosely, Brianna and Michael Simmons, thank you for your sweet innocence, love and natural inspiration. "Always do your very best, be phenomenal".

Thank you to my Aunt Sylvia (my namesake), a foxy lady with a sassy flare.

Thank you so graciously to my dear friend Cassandra Rene', you have walked this literary journey with me daily and I appreciate your love.

Thank you to my dear friend Tenecia Moncrief-Williams, my guardian angel. "Beyond the true meaning of 'friend'", I appreciate your love.

Thank you to Kwame Alexander for his direction and optimistic insight in publishing this book and for the layout design. Here's to Do The Write Thing. Your creative ambition is intriguing.

A warm hearty thank you to four gentleman, Bro Ah and the Jazz Collectors, Baba Bisa, Alex Leak and Mike Peay for the broadcast promotions, inspirations, love, kindness, cultural creativity and support.

Thank you to all my sisters in FEW, Inc., especially Allie Latimer, Esquire, Janie Taylor, Yvonne Duncan, Debbie Terrell, Karen Saunders, Sandra Canery, Arlene Cooper, Jeaneatte Miller, Jane Morgan, the late Doris Douglas and the late Audrey Best, for their strength, pride, encouragement and love.

To my friends and fellow poets Doris and Perry Little, thank you for sharing and thank you for your love.

Thank you with love and appreciation, to the clergy in my life, especially my pastor, Fr. Butta, Fr. Michael Salah,

Fr. Bob Guillen, Fr. David Bava and Fr. Innocent Njoku, God bless you always.

Thank you to Sr. Bridgid and Sr. Margarett of St. Francis Xaiver Catholic Church, for your love and encouragement.

Looking over the roving years, reflecting on a strong, righteous, courageous foundation, I thank my kindergarten teacher Mrs. Cook and my second grade teacher Mrs. Battle, Garfield Elementary School, Southeast, Washington, D.C., my fourth grade teacher, the late, Sr. Mary Agnesine, Our Lady of Perpetual Help Catholic School, Southeast, Washington, D.C., Mr. Vowels, seventh and eight grade English and French teacher, the late, Mr. Attrus Fleming, ninth grade music teacher, both of Kramer Jr. High School, Mr. Page, eleventh grade Driver's Education teacher and Mr. Sloan, twelfth grade Math teacher both of Anacostia High School, Southeast, Washington, D.C.

Thank you so kindly to my friends Rose Valraie, Sheryl Cohen, C. Rene' Calloway, Roosevelt Cain, Jr., Glenn Harris, the late Valerie A. Dorsey, Chris Hill-Gray, Deidra Gray, Abena Disroe, Natalie Johnson, C. Jeanean Gibbs, Angela Owens, Danny Queen, Michael Butler, E. Ethelbert Miller, Curtis T. White, Esq., Sharon Hurd, Demetrius Merritt, Regena Bromery, Ginger Clark, Diana Cox, Marie Clarke, Bill Black, Carolyn "Black Beauty" Providence, Pluria W. Marshall, Derrick Humphries, Esq., Jerry Thomas, Jr., Esquire, Thomas G. Krattenmaker, Esq., Sonya Hatchet, Estelle Brown, Dorothy and Tommy Waters, Virginia Akers, Laura Toler, Denise Ladson, Jeanette Fields, Jay Johnson, J. Ford, Michelle Wright,

Jamala Snead, Linda Hagans, Sharah Jones, Michael and Lisa Brown and Just-Asia Scott, friends are treasured gifts from God.

Thanks to my Godchildren Lisa Brice-Goodman, Gregory Gaines, Jr., Andrew Stevens, Sophia Michelle and Anya Cherie Leonard who I've share many hours of joy. Your presence in my life has added to my happiness.

Thanks to my nephew Brandon T. Carter for the mental challenge and stimulation with backgammon, you amaze me! A wondrous thank you to my nephew, Jabari Beverly for sharing his artistic creativity. Here's to my partner, my friend, my nephew, my Scrabble partner and my challenge, Korin Dawud Agnew for the many hours of shared joy. Thank you to my niece Shamis Beverly for sharing her artistic talents and for sharing a mutual interest in reading, handwriting, diction, and especially "Scrabble". A hearty thanks to all my nephews, Dione, Daniel, Garikai, Daudi, Kebo, Issa, Hemonse, Tony, JR., Christopher, Wahsuphansefwah and Ramumensaunk, "continue to be gentlemen". My dear nieces, Ronke', Maia, Dayo, the late "Sweet Rashida", Habibah, Yazmina, Ayana, Tonia, Amenhefent, Hetepusamut, Bernadette and Jessica. I'm thanking you perpetually for your love and admiration, stay beautiful and sweet, "keep your head to the sky and your eyes on the prize."

Thank you to all my family and friends, by the grace of God, too numerous to mention by name. Feel it, you know who you are.

Peace, prayer, love and blessings.

Sylvia Dianne Beverly

Contents

Introduction

On a clear, crisp, cold winter morning in January, the year nineteen hundred and ninety-three, I sat around the round table with my parents, at their home, watching the inaugural events and waiting for what would turn out, for me, to be the highlight of all inaugurations. Dr. Maya Angelou had been chosen by President-Elect William Jefferson Clinton to write and present an inaugural poem. Dr. Maya Angelou delivered with poise, confidence and conviction, "On the Pulse of Morning". This poem is filled with spirituality, nature, love, reality, strength and the love and goodness of mankind. Wondrously, Dr. Angelou constructed this poem by using three elements, "a rock, a river, a tree"...taken from old Negro spirituals, back to nature, a wholesome foundation of strength for the President of the United States.

Not since the late President John Fitzgerald Kennedy, had a president extended this honor to a poet, when President Kennedy afforded the opportunity to Robert Frost in nineteen hundred sixty-three. Words alone could never capture how ecstatic I was for this occasion and the outstanding recognition of my all time favorite, writer, poet, and heroine. I was touched greatly. Ever since I read "I Know Why the Caged Bird Sings", I have been a fan of Dr.

Maya Angelou. I had read most of her autobiographies and with each, enjoyed and admired the way Dr. Maya Angelou shared her life so openly, presenting ultimate strength in overcoming obstacles of life's toils, trials and tribulations. At this time, I decided to compile my poetry and form a book entitled "Forever In Your Eyes", paying tribute to many and dedicated to Dr. Maya Angelou.

After the blessing of hearing Oprah Winfrey recite, in person, Dr. Maya Angelou's "Phenomenal Woman", I was determined to make a part of me, some of Dr. Maya Angelou's poetry. I chose "Phenomenal Woman" first and over the past decade many; many folks have enjoyed my dramatic presentation of "Phenomenal Woman". I enjoy reciting Dr. Maya Angelou's poetry to the utmost, but I have also grown to the likeness of reciting original poetry including the poem "Forever In Your Eyes". You will find my poetry consist of real live situations, coupled with much love, sincere appreciation, numerous tributes, superb love of nature and spirituality. Each poem is written with special intentions of personal expression. I pray there is a poem here for all to enjoy. We have waited patiently for the creation of "Forever In Your Eyes", through faith we visualize its birth. All that I do is by the grace of God. To God Be The Glory.

Sylvia Dianne Beverly

Foreword

Sylvia Dianne Beverly approached me to write the forward to her book "Forever In Your Eyes" when I, as a former educationist, had already served as South African Ambassador to the United States for nearly four years and at a time, or so I believed, when I had evolved into a thoroughly political animal. Accustomed as I had become to addressing audiences at the drop of a hat on any number of matters, immersed as I was in issues, issues, issues, I was not sure that this would be a task easily handled. I was surprised, or rather my thought processes were taken by surprise when I began to tackle this project-not by the differences in approach that were called for, but rather by the similarities between my work and Sylvia's own brand of creativity.

As a matter of fact, this is when my teacher's brain clicked into overdrive and my teacher's heart began to thump. I saw the link, the connection and I was able to reconcile not only my two selves, but also the seemingly opposite worlds of politics and art.

I make no pretense of being a literary philosopher, but I hope you will forgive my enjoyment at seeing how Ms. Beverly's work reflects the America I have come to know from my own travels and through countless discussions, interactions and observations.

I have had the kindred need to probe, to question and to reflect my own environment in a vibrant, fresh, tangible, and convincing way. Words and what they must convey have been my focus-the center of my existence.

Upon reading Sylvia Dianne Beverly's work, you will be struck by her close association with her subjects. It is striking to me how the author, herself, or at least her essence, flows through the work. There is a sense that there is a fundamental truthful unity in the world and the spirit of Sylvia Dianne Beverly is undoubtedly one of the binding forces.

One of the author's favorite words is "Phenomenal." For me, the use is distinctive because it exemplifies her enthusiasm and high energy. The positive, encouraging, hopeful, far- and outreaching connotations of this single word can also easily be translated to a definition for the essence of the author's work. For this reason, I could not help, but smile when I learned that Sylvia Dianne Beverly is well known as the "Love Poet."

My favorite poem, and you will allow me this personal and professional favoritism, I hope, is entitled "Education." It is an exercise in combining the theory of words and their inherent meanings with real time interaction and participation. This poem is incomplete on paper-it requires, no, it stipulates, human voices and interaction to come fully into existence. I like that. For me, that is why we write or create in the first place. Art, to like-and when it manages to acknowledge and celebrate its source to this extent, I can only say "Bravo!" It is my sincere hope that you will enjoy this work as much as I have and that you will refer to it repeatedly whenever you feel a little in need of a human touch.

Franklin A. Sonn

Forever In Your Eyes

poems

Let This Dream Come True
10/89

Friends, Americans Congresspersons,
Lend me your ears.
Households should be headed by a man.
The world would be a better place to live.
Children would have positive influence from
both parents.
Parents sharing work...makes a stronger foundation
for our children.

I dream of world without single family homes.
No Mr. Mom...No Mommy playing Daddy.
I dream of world where the Father is strong provider
Where Mother nurtures family daily.

I dream of world where every family
has strong male dominance.
Instill seriousness, self-confidence, responsibility,
pride and wisdom in our children.

Through the grace of God all children know Jesus.
Through the grace of God all children know
how to say their prayers at bedtime, kneel on their
knees and fold their hands.
Through the grace of God all children know
what it is to say blessings before meals, give thanks
for food to become nourished and healthy.

I dream of world...when children enter school
they project manners and discipline.
When children enter school...they are ready to learn
and put forth their best efforts. They are creative and
willing to succeed. They receive both academics and
technical aspects of studies.
They receive spiritual and religious teachings
and guidance.   ˙

Dreams do come true; dreams do come true, yes,
dreams do come true.
Let this dream be made a reality.
Mothers do not run off to work leaving the children
to send themselves to school.
Mothers are able to be full-time mothers again,
devote time towards baking, play games with and
nurture children tenderly through their childhood.
Fathers will be a distinctive structure in the home,
creating a more sound financial structure.
Children can free their minds of questions such as
"I wonder where my Dad is living" or
"Will my Daddy ever come home again?"

I dream of world where the nation is free from
Negative encounters, dwells on positive solutions,
promotes construction and shun destruction.

May nurturing from all mothers instill righteous ways
for our children.

Let our children know, fun is good,
It is always better to tell the truth
Love is best and will conquer all.
This dream makes for a better world.

Blood is Thicker Than Mud
4/8/04

Great-grand Dad and
Grandmother told us long time ago
Mom Dad reminded us through years too
Let it be said, to thy own self be true...
We say it to each other
All we really have is one another
Your life water and mine flow from same veins
Like a Girl Scout's pack
Like a pin pals prick
Like women perpetually stick together thing
Until the end of time-no matter what-
We may not always agree, at very least
We come to the meeting at the round table
Reconcile for Peace
Forever and always you will be mine
Dear Sister of mine...the sun will forever shine
Is there really a pot-of-gold at rainbow's end?
Remember how we said through thick and thin
We would always be friends
We would dress alike...I know you can not forget
Our Supremes' Act
Some things are just too fun not to treasure
We need to stick together beyond measure
Join in with a strong union and not go astray
Let us continue to pray these troubles away
One day...one mighty fine day...this too shall past
There is no way this madness will last

We will come around...with forgiveness,
kisses and hugs
We will remember our ancestors' words
"blood is thicker than mud."

Sincere Thunder
8/16/94

Call to your spirit, conga's are keen...
Your words echo bold and serene.

"Dry your eyes loved ones, my dear friends,
wipe away mundane tears."

"Rejoice...celebrate my arrival to that glorious plane."

I am proud to have shared with you the best I can
Hope when I was no longer needed on this planet,
each would carry on as you should.

It is most evident my spirituality exists...
For a while I have been waiting, for everlasting
happiness.

Consistently taking on responsibilities...
Accomplish each level of education for acquired
knowledge within.

Made a part of me words our ancestors sing...
Share with audiences, expressions from Robeson to
Shakespeare...entertain over and over again.

Cease high-pitched wining
Breathe deep...let thunder rumble...
Hear the chant?

Quite meticulous...except no less than perfection.

A heart so kind, warm and tender
Lend a helping hand...that is what I want
you to remember.

Appease yourself...You know best what you like...
"Remember I am Sincere."

*(In memory of Douglas M. Johnson,
a.k.a. "Sincere Thunder Namefree")*

Highest Regard
(Haiku # 1)

Darling because of
you, everything in my
life is more cherished.

Someone Cares
2/14/97

So sweet and thoughtful always true
Folks around can depend on you.

Outspoken in words, quick to ask why
Quite a surprise...you can actually be shy.

Unique in character, being a lady is in
I feel blessed having you as my friend.

Remember wholeheartedly...unity prevails
It always helps, knowing someone else cares.

God is on our side, all we have to do
Acknowledge His presence
His strength shines through.

Life is hard, most times pretty fair
Continue to show one another someone cares.

(Dedicated to LaTashia)

Edu-cation
3/10/97

When I say edu - you say cation!
Edu - cation! Edu - cation!

A little girl told me, just the other day
Make your poem a rap, then the children
will listen to what you have to say.

Do all you can do to stay in school
Don't be a looser...Please don't be no fool.
Edu - cation! Edu - cation!

Get your clothes ready the night before
Check all that you need, rest, breakfast, books
before you walk out the door.

Start out young...Plan to be a success
Let it show each day, in the way you dress.

Make sure education is yours to get
Without it, through life, you will fret.
Edu - cation! Edu - cation!

Keep prayer in your heart, body, mind and soul
Read your Bible... It's where the beginning story is told.
Edu - cation! Edu - cation! Edu - cation!
Stay in School! Peace...Out!
(For Bernadette and all our youth)

Beautiful Beginnings
(Haiku #2)

Beginnings are beau-
tiful...now reminiscing
on the day we met.

Mystic Change
(Haiku # 13) 11/3/02

You said there's nothing
You would change about me somehow
Change comes any old way.

Be Unto Me

I'm as happy as a nightingale
As content as I can be
Just finished listening to the
Words of Christ,
"Be Unto ME."

Woman With A Mission

Recognize a need...
Analyze to the utmost,
  an astonishing breed.
Elaborate on the essentials of
  acquired deeds...
Accept the barriers and challenges of
  life's needs.
Struggle onward steadfast...
Move toward the future, yet glance
  at the past
Study history to gain knowledge to share...
Know without knowledge, you would be minus a care.
Strive toward goals, arrive at success.
Emphasis on the positive...do not dwell on the rest...
Never give up because you are committed and true...
Flourish with smiles and radiance, that is you.
A woman with a mission.

(Dedicated to Joy)

Desirous Love

Wonder deeply what a true love would bring.

Feel the goodness of being loved tenderly

Everlasting togetherness.

Make a life of fun, A life of love and laughter.

Enjoy to the utmost, the sharing and caring

of one another. True love our greatest desire.

Love will conquer all.

(For Billye)

Precious Time

Time waits for no man...
We are either in front of it or behind...
Sometimes we hit it right on time.

Right on time...
That is the way it is whenever we get together...
I enjoy ...I appreciate the time...

Don't ever want to take precious time for granted.

It is great fate and fortune we met
Our association is unique within it.

What we have other than being friends...
We know where the action begins
We know where it ends.

Uniquely you are my most inspiring good friend.

You are in my heart, my mind, my soul...
Until my fate with precious time ends.

(For Pluria)

Extremes

Dark, subtle, an aura of love
Holding hands enjoying the flight of
birds above.

Walking by the waters, stopping often
to embrace
Feeling lighthearted....like fragrant
Wisp of elegant lace.

Oh my heart is so heavy tonight
Through my tears I feel it is just not right.

Casual and polite to one another
Oh Darling our passion goes much, much further.

Just a few days ago - childhood games were our play
Now in dead silence, by my side you lay.

I know with prayer, our indifferences will cease
I wish it were before we go to sleep, at least.

Thought I would mention this infinite extreme
With an aura of love, I hold fast to our dream.

I hold fast to our dream
Talk about extremes.

Trust in Him Fondly
2/26/98

Anchor our love in God each day
Trust in Him fondly along life's way.

Be like a tree planted by the water
Spread your wings with much confidence you
Will not falter.

Blessed are you who are hungry...you will be fed
Extend love and life to others
By doing so, down the right path you are led.

Recognize, many do not have as much as we
But for the grace of God, truly goes thee.

God's way is so powerful, much above ground
So happy to have prayer and know love's been found.

Rejoice, rejoice, distress not over earthly possessions
Know our biggest reward comes once we reach
Heaven.
Change, change our attitude, change our way
Ask for Jesus' help in prayer, each night and day.

Trust in Him fondly, give away our worst fears
Trust in Him fondly, we will have everlasting love
through the years. Alleluia!
(Dedicated to Father Innocent Njoku)

Love: A Many Splendid Thing

Love is a many splendid thing
Fills you with delight, makes your heart sing.

So much goodness throughout the day
Makes you feel encouraged as you go your merry way.

Someone to watch over you in all that you do
Share each moment, so splendid so wonderfully true.

There is nothing you can't accomplish with ecstatic
delight
A wholehearted, encouraged, strong-willed might.

Open your heart, let the sun shine in
Do it, just do it, you are sure to win.

Love is a many, many splendid thing!

(Written in London, England 3-11-98)

Circus Days
3/21/97

The circus is coming, the circus is coming
They say its the "greatest show on earth."
Have you ever wondered why the people
of the circus give us their mighty worth?

The cheerful ring master with his tall, black top hat
and supportive fancy cane,
Helps to keep it all together in a big voice
one act after another he excitedly brings.

The clowns in their colorful outfits,
Dance and parade around,
Some with big, smiling, happy faces and
some with a sad, sad frown.

They do tricks and play jokes on each other
just to make
the children and grown folks laugh
It's no wonder the circus comes to town each Spring,
It's no wonder its a gas.

Popcorn, peanuts and cotton candy too
It's so much fun and goodness at the circus,
Super fun for me and super fun for you.

Many exciting parts and great,
great things to do and see

Which is your favorite thing at the circus,
What's your favorite way to be?

How about the tigers and lions,
as we watch the brave trainers in their cage
Or would your favorite be the team
of brothers hopping the tight rope on one leg?

Keep in mind that the circus will be here
soon and very soon
You just may want to take a friend,
someone less fortunate than you.

Remember kind children, may all your days be
circus days,
Happy, Fun and Smiling as you go your merry way.

(For the students of West Elementary School,
Washington, D.C.)

Forever In Your Eyes

Phenomenal, even though you've described
Yourself as same
It starts with the sweetness of the sound
of your name.

You have a style of elegance that surfaces
with each work that you master
I'm touched by your emotions
now and forever after.

Fantastic to see you receive
the recognition deserved
More than two decades that the
"Caged Bird" has been preserved.

Charity, justice, equality above all
It's no wonder you were a distinguished guest
at the inaugural ball.

Extraordinary expression as to what pride
can do for you
With a constant struggle and belief in all that
you strive to do.

Life is a constant battle and
we know that's no lie
I can feel it Maya, I can see it,
that's why those tears are forever in your eyes.

I Cry
8/30/03

I cried
I had to cry
I lost the love of my life
I know the goodness of love because of him
I feel the power of the Holy Spirit because
Of our love and unity
I cherish many glad glorious memories shared
Grace our spirits
I appreciate our outward expressions of love
For one another
I love the way we always loved each other
I love how we expressed our love to each other,
Often and always
Oh...my handsome Knight, I love you handsome King
I love you with a mighty might
I will always love you
I love how I can still hear you say
"I love you too Bae!"
I will always miss you.
I will always have a reason to cry
I hurt
So...I cry.

*(Dedicated to the Loving Memory and Great Honor
of the late Daniel Levi Beverly, Jr.)*

Real Love
11/15/03

I really love you Baby
I love you in all seasons
I love you in Winter Baby
I love when we cuddle by the fireplace
  And watch Jeopardy on TV
I love how we put away our lightweight
  Clothes and bring out the warm
I love you in all seasons
I love you in Spring Baby
I love how we plant flowers, sit on the
  Patio, watch the flowers grow
I love the smell of cherry blossoms so sweet
I love how we prepare for Easter, Holy Thursday,
  Good Friday and especially shopping for that
  Easter Bonnet with all the frills upon it.
I really love you Baby.
I love you in all seasons
I love you in Summer Baby
I love walks by the water holding hands together
I love going to the beach and laying in the sun
I love how each weekend we cannot wait to get
  Out of town, have some fun
I really love you Baby.
I love you in all seasons
I love you in Fall Baby
I love how we begin to start all over again
I love how the wind blows lightly through my hair

I love exotic smell of logs on fire and just
  Knowing you are there
I love how it turns dark a bit early
  (Night time is the right time)
I really love you Baby
I love you in all seasons
I love you day and night
I love you and your love for me is the reason
I really love you Baby!

Artist Baby!!!
7/6/98

You are an artist Baby
Face it, it's a fact...
  it's no dog-gone maybe.
Sharing and promoting talent near and far
Across nations you are a genuine star.
Not just on the weekly radio airwaves
But here and there, we find you on stage.
Artist Baby!!!
You have a natural, mystical, magical
rhythm and beat
Listen to the melodic sounds of your flute
so sweet.
Your conga drums and kungas add extra
pulsating vibes
Helps to keep deeply the spoken word alive.
Perpetually networking, supporting and
promoting new artist
We shall always remember you and
the mastery of talent you've brought us.
Artist Baby!!!
Love is a many splendid thing
Let it fill your heart as you continue to sing...
Yes, You Are An Artist Baby!!!

(Dedicated to Bro. Ah)

Everlasting Light of Life
9/16/93

Smooth, soothing, masculine voice, echoes in my ears
I can still feel the warmth of the oil lamp that
penetrates my soul and prevails light far and near.

Warm and bright, wonderfully true, Amazing light
Comforts my being, throughout my life.
Yes.....the Everlasting Light of Life.

Guides me in directions of great height beaming light
Shining with a steady flow of greatness for all my life.

Never failing, always prevailing masterful light
Supporting encounters put before me a test
of my integrity.
Everlasting Light of Life.

One phase of accomplishments, trailing another
encouraging light
Never ending feelings, penetrating each aspiration.

Remember the warmth of
the oil lamp's glow of eternal light
Present during my joyful birth and promoting
wondrous success in life.
Smile on the Everlasting Light of Life.

(A dedication for James Earl Jones)

No Ordinary Brother
9/2/98

You are a quality man the company we've
grown accustomed to
A dedicated, gracious gentleman with
immaculate style of GQ.

Always erect, strong and firm
your ever-loving stance
Walking across the room with the command
of an instructor of dance.

That's why I say "you're no ordinary brother".

Immersed in issues, issues and issues,
around the world
Yet you take time to help mankind, your fellow
man, woman, boy and girl.

Tackle each project as if it were truly your own
Leaving your recipients with feelings we all wish
to have known.

Caring for each, like "no ordinary brother".

Humble and delightful with appreciation for whatever
you are given
Share your wisdom for the acquired knowledge within.

Expressing deep passions with
a heartbeat of love and sincerity
Comforting with words of hope,
affording support, a manner that is carefree.

Creating an environment that is tangible, vibrant, fresh
and most convincing
Conditions of wonderment, like a morning glory's dew
brilliant and glistening.

Down to earth, masterly articulate and skillfully
artistic, "no ordinary brother".

*(Dedicated to Franklin A. Sonn, South African
Ambassador to the United States of America)*

A Tribute To Maya

To a Husband", "They ask Why",
Seven Women's Blessed Assurance",
"They Went Home", "Phenomenal Women",
"And Still I Rise"
A few favorites I share
often with inquisitive eyes.

Of course these are only a few
from the many works of your creative mind.
I only wish to meet, in person,
the master of mystic and a long time favorite
of mine.

Waiting to meet your acquaintance and spend
Some time with faith, hope and love
knowing its soon to come to me
with blessings from above.

Wild And Crazy

Your Crazy... makes my crazy...
not seem so crazy.
Yes, Wild and Crazy.

Fun and free, sincere and good,
being all you can be.

Challenging at best,
forgetting the rest.

Optimistic views...
relief from the blues.
Wild and Crazy.

Footloose and fancy free...
a long way from any commitment to me.
Wild and Crazy.

You make my heart sing...
With each notion that you bring
is oh...so...
Wild and Crazy.

(Dedicated to Darrell E. Patterson)

A Tribute for Gordon Parks
11-22-97

Tears roll down my face...Oh I don't know why
I guess I'm just so happy for you,
so happy to come to see you
Then you walked by.

A standing ovation, even before the first sound
of the keys
Then sweet melodic sound filled with jubilee.

Silence, deep silence wondering yearning
in awe of more
Our undivided attention, a legend before
our eyes in creative statue, you score.

So exciting, amazing your wonderful style
It's no wonder at first glance
I throw you kisses with a delightful broad smile.

Can't wait for the conclusion to acknowledge what's
heaven sent
Each concerto and sonata is what my existence
has meant.

We are all filled with emotion of your expression of
family peace
Not forgetting the rapture of rolling
and roaring black and white keys.

Remind us of the rolling tears
Remind us of the chaos, turmoil and

our deepest fears
Turmoil interrupts our best years.
BRAVO!

Blessings of Existence
1-13-97

On a cold Winter's night
The wind howls with a fierce might

Kneeling in prayer to God
our Heavenly Love
Waking in the morning to snow
white as a Dove.

Truly in God's name we pray
Thank you for the blessings received each
and every day.

Blessings of existence, bestowed upon you
It's your Birthday! Happy to share with you
so true.

*(Dedicated to My Priest, My Confidant, My Friend
Father Bob's 59th Birthday)*

A Phenomenal Blessing
9/2/98

A phenomenal blessing
an intricate part of life always
Encourage and share
with many thoroughly with passing days.

Enjoy the compositions of tributes and love
Appreciative of the creative blessings from
heaven above.

Thrilled by smiles of wide-eyed fans
Hope they realize I always give the best I can.

Take nothing for granted about this special creativity
Blessings continue to flow, bringing us more and
more poetry.

What A Phenomenal Blessing!

(Dedicated to Fellow Poets and Poetess)

Listen To Your Heart
3-9-99

Let your heart talk to you good people
Let it ring to the highest steeple.

God is everywhere and He's talking to you too
Listen to the inner voices, let His holiness
shine through.

Be ever mindful of His tremendous sacrifice
By doing so, you will acquire everlasting life.

Listen to your heart...through trials and
Tribulations you'll sing
Listen...listen to your heart in heaven and
on earth, let freedom ring.

Let your heart talk to you, It's God's voice you hear
Listen, take heed it's God's voice loud and clear.

(Dedicated to Fr. Innocent Njoku)

Deep Sadness
2/5/99

Sadness in my heart surfaces....

Deep sadness that takes over the

core of my being....

Sadness erased by prayer....affording

my life a deeper meaning.

Deep....deep sadness.

I'm so happy prayer won't let you be.

A Plead for Salvation
3-9-99

Listen, listen to what your heart is saying
Listen, intently to the cries from which we are swaying.

Unite in the name of the Lord, wipe away all prejudice
Lend a helping hand, volunteer to save face of
all races.

Falling on our knees in sacrifice and prayer
Have mercy on those who lend service for our care.

Prayer is so powerful it expresses our need
Prayer is the salvation of our greatest plead.

There's much to be done and many to sustain
Prayer is so powerful it eliminates the pain.

Easier said than done, its surely a challenge for all
Unite with one another, hear this plead, hear this call.

Have no fear, my friend, just come on board
Give back in thanksgiving, truly trust in the Lord.

Trust in Him fondly it's our greatest plead
Our plead for salvation, it's our greatest need.

(Dedicated to Fr. Innocent)

Magnificent Man
3/1/97

Magnificent Man, oh, so ecstatic
to have known a few
Greetings always with a warm smile
and gentle embrace for you.

Your presence alone gives off electrifying security
Keeping us "everlastingly" informed of current events
and history!

Magnificent Man, sitting around the round table
with peace and earnesty.
Sheerly a grand feeling for family and for me.

Talking about jazz "Lemon Tree" and the
high-back chair...
fond memories perpetually
One hundred percent committed, always listens,
year after year, with love unconditionally.

Magnificent Man, realistically proud, spiritual and true
A shining example always, for our youth to look up to.

Extending services to many, near and far
You place a gleam in our eyes forevermore...
"you're a shining star".

Flavored with a big heart of no nonsense

Yet, a man of humor, honor, laughter and wit.

Magnificent Man, we see strength and courage
with a mere glance towards you
Always lending a helping hand with a gentleman's
style so true.

Yes, you're a Magnificent Man
And my life is better for I've perpetually known you
Magnificent, Magnificent, Magnificent Man,
that's you.

(Dedicated to the late Joseph Albert Brawner, Sr.)

My Dearest Darling Mother
5/9/96

True blessings for the love we share
Your caring and nurturing has always
been there.

You taught me to always do what is right
To pray to God with a righteous might.

Know prayer changes things
Even when it is cloudy, the goodness of
Sunshine it brings.

Each and every day
With thanksgiving I pray
To be more and more like you
So kind, spiritual, wonderful and true.

Your radiant smile and graceful style
Give a very special touch
to the things we love so much.

Baking, fund raising, CCD, Sodality,
Husband, Children, Grandchildren,
Sisters, Brothers, Other family...
Friends, neighbors and associates
are a consistent few.
All the love and happiness you give
May it always come back to you.

If ever there were an angel on earth
My Dearest Darling Mother
Let it be known, your sweet love I have
enjoyed since birth.

(For Dorothy)

You're A Classic
5/27/96

To preserve your unique style
Would aid young men and make their
living in the future, worthwhile.
Your strong love and dedication is
beyond consistent
When you speak or laugh, we all stop
and readily listen.

You're definitely a classic.

Touching many more lives than you can imagine
Young men have followed your unique pattern
Taking consistent great care of nine children
and your wife
Gives each of us memories of joy, love
and blessings throughout the rest of our life.

You're definitely a classic.

Providing us with the best life has to offer
Working around the clock without a falter.
With a fetish for clocks and watches
No wonder you're always on time,
accepting no excuses.

Bet on it Dad...you're a classic.

Helping to look after your grandchildren as well
Sitting in your company, waiting on the story
you'd tell.
Planning to celebrate whatever the occasion
Setting up a menu with love, then stating
"is everybody happy?"

You're a classic, Dad!

Love all the innocent babies in a caring way
Wish they could stay small and ready for play
Guide us and teach us with dignity and pride
Being Dad's Little Girl, I wouldn't trade, even
for a roller-coaster ride.

Such a classic.

Your romanticism and sentimental acts
Alerts the same flow for our family and
Dad, that is a fact.
Pretty wrapped packages, candy, ice cream and flowers
Surprises and love songs for that special hour.

You're a classic.

The emphasis you place on a good writing pen
Assist with my blessings, for me writing is in.
Stand tall and be proud
While I shout out loud
Here's to the grandest Dad of all,

.Happy Father's Day.
Yes, You're a Classic.

*(Dedicated to the late Daniel Levi Beverly, Sr. Father's
Day, June 16, 1996)*

Deep In My Heart
6/20/99

Dad....My heart over-flowed with
true love
You filled it....my heart, like a
warm heavenly cove.

Sweet loving memories of the way
you would sing
Comforting our home with melodic sounds
...you are King.

Strong and fearless, your love ones
always protected
Yet gentle and caring, no kin
ever rejected.

Deep in my heart lies the love you gave
and I stored
So much love Dad, it will continue to
fill my life forevermore.

So much love!

*(Dedicated in Memory of the late Daniel Levi Beverly, Sr.
Father's Day '99)*

Back To Nature
10/7/98

Back to nature, green grass, blue skies
Music playing softly in the background
The blues, jazzy blues, camouflage Mama's cries.

Back to nature, beautiful green grass and
tall, sturdy trees
Blowing below the blue blanket of our
magnificent skies...a cool fall breeze.

Relaxing on the front porch, blue violets
and lilacs fragrantly sweet, after the rain
Knowledge of street crime and youths being
shot down, outrage from a community
continuously filled with pain.

Determined to turn the blues
into serene, tranquil, peaceful nights
Take out quality time for those who are lost,
green and filled with fright.

Back to nature, is where we must go to get a firm grip
Wise historians, true scholars, working diligently
to eliminate the blues under the new millennium's
counseled tip.

Back to nature, enjoyment in watching the blue
waters of the Caribbean

Sail and water ski, looking out at the horizon
Sweet aquamarine.

Express true blue, tremendous concern for our
children's future
Afford hands on experience, develope stage
presence with public speaking lectures.

Compassion, sensitivity, comfort and
concernment
Especially interested in our youth's
healthy green nutriment.

Back to nature, a royal blue, lily-of-the-fields,
tranquilled paradise
Back to nature, a forest of green pine, whether
jade or emerald, we continue to rise.

Sunshine, blue skies, rainbows and butterflies
BACK TO NATURE, yes, BACK TO NATURE!!!!!!

*(Dedicated to Michael Peay, Esquire, Jazz Collector,
WPFW Radio)*

Love's Been Here All the Time

Love's been here, yeah man all the time
You were the furthest being from my mind.

I looked at you darling and I said oh no
Then I thought again and said oooo Baby maybe so.

Love's been here all the time.

Surely a handsome, gallant knight, perhaps
its that smile of delight
Coupled with dimples and a determined might.

Or just the inspiration and wisdom received
Spending time with you fills a great need.
You know Honey, you're a rare breed.

Love's been here all the time.

True love, a blessing from heaven above
Pure as the likeness of a graceful dove
What I feel for you now is appreciation
and love.

A lifetime of being single
Thought I couldn't find Mr. Right
Now mattering how often I mingle
once a year or every night.

Oh my Darling Love....love's been here all the time.

Now that we have committed,
I'm sure true love is in it.

Isn't it just great,
We are so happy, we are wonderful soul mates.

Dreaming and singing the same tune
Yes...yes, My Sweet Darling I'll be your
lovely bride real soon.

Love's been here all the time,
It's been here all the time,
I'm so happy you're mine
Love...Love...Love...Love Darling
It's been here all the time.

(Dedicated to Darrell E. Patterson)

Three Generations
11/22/97

"Come my grandson, come my Dear and go with me
Today I've accepted an invitation to hear the
National Symphony!"
"What will that consist of Grandmommy, just what
will it be?"

"It's history in the making at the Kennedy Center
Witnessing a living legend with the great Gordon Parks
presenting".

"Grandmommy, that sounds exciting, I'd like to go
A Black man in the 'lime-light' and its not about
Sport's ego."

"Lets be adventurous and ride the bus and subway
Then walk in the night rain to Auntie closing out
the work day."

"That sounds great, but Grandmommy is it your fate
Or should we go Auntie's way and check the
taxi-rate?"

"We can make it, thank you my Dear
As long as we pray and keep our Savior near."

"I'm happy to be with you Grandmommy,
as happy as I can be

My joy will be a phenomenal experience tonight...
once we see Mr. Parks, what a grand jubilee."

Arriving long before the doors open without haste
Giving rapid proceeding toward eliminating any
rat race.

Fantastic seats up close in the front orchestra
A unique outing for all ages to witness a living legend
without flaw.

Happy, happy, happy to sheer ecstasy
Keeping our youth close to us, real close
Helps to make life more gleeful....more gleefully.

(Dedicated to Dorothy E. Beverly and Brandon T. Carter)

For The Love of Admiration
2/2/97

My Godmother, My Aunt, My Comrade without strife
One to be admired, highly influential throughout my
entire life.

Everlasting dignity, a lady with class in abundance
Sharing often with many...celebrations of food, song
and dance.

Ex out procrastination, get on with details
No time to waste "won't want to miss the ship's sails."

Practice earnestly, penmanship, please don't
forget proper manners and diction
Exaggerating at times to emphasize reality,
eliminating fiction.

Collector of fine materials...an honorable
Display of beauty of gorgeous gems and stones
Setting down to hand painted linen...a magnificent
attraction on its own.

Documented as a woman to be admired in
Prince George's County
Enough credits to her name, justifying
International bounty.

Working consistently for family, friends, job

and community
Not recognizing the impact is sheer beauty.

A strong determined might of perfection
A perpetual deep love of admiration.

(Dedicated to Mary Azalia Brawner, my Godmother)

Fancy Mellow Fellow
6/26/03

Fancy Fellow...Weeping Willow
Fluffy wisps of nature's pillow
Marvelous maple tree...yummy sweet
Waiting for earnest, eager eyes
And special smiles to meet
Thought him was a Fancy Fellow
Oh so mellow, until he fell into
A pool of yellow jell-o.

(For Forestine)

Nice
3/22/99

A kind, sweet, endearing heart
Organization from the start
Commitment to each other,
surely staying together
Nice
Sweet and nice.

Looking after our elders
Planning special occasions
Answering invitations
Attending special events
Nice
Wonderful and nice.

Volunteer worker
Making sacrifice
Working with the Missionary
Encouraging others to give
Helping the less fortunate to live
Nice
Courageous and nice.

Sending a cheerful note
Making a phone call just to say hello
Remembering friends and
loved ones with flowers
Baking a cake to celebrate the hour

Nice
Oh so special and nice.

Attending church services
Singing in the choir
Teaching Sunday school
Participating in bible study and renew
Nice
Spiritual and nice.

Motivational presentations
Righteous influence
Sharing information
Adding a touch of poetry
Nice
Delightful and nice...Be nice.

(Dedicated to Dorothy E. Beverly)

Smile
6/24/03

God is truly wonderful.
Whatever it is give it to Him.
God will show the way.
He will show the right way.
God is always around
He is everywhere
No matter the hour
No matter the reason
No matter the season
Always God is there for us
So let us smile
Forever be true
Forever God will there for
Me and You.

*(Dedicated to the Youth of Greater Mt. Nebo
Summer Youth Program)*

#One Fan
3/31/03

I love to see your face
Peeking at me through my Kindergarten Class door
Each time I vision your beautiful face
Blended with your wonderfully kind spirit
Makes me love you that much more.

I love how you always say what you mean
And mean what you say
Oh so much
Speaking quiet words of substance and truth
Never engaging in just such and such.

I love so much about you
You are truly dear to my heart
A phenomenal role model, my hero,
In my corner from the very start.

I love you so,
I want the whole wide world to know
I love how you always told me to hold close To me
Three virtues, yes, Faith, Hope and Charity
Oh the greatest, yes is Charity
Which is Love, That's what you are
Lucrative Love and Love is my #One Fan.

*(Dedicated to Dorothy E. Beverly - My Mother,
My #One Fan)*

Mama Sweetie
5/8/04

Mama...I smile when I first see you,
Cause you are made that way
Mama...your smile is so tender, sweetly beautiful
Forever and a day
Mama Sweetie...you have a devotion of your self
Unconditionally
Always here for all your children, grandchildren
Great-grands as well...to teach...to share
Daily...prayerfully...show each of us you care
Provide and guide us toward a righteous spiritual
Life...the way God our Father wants us to live
Teach by example has perpetually been your style
A pleasure to spend time with you
Everlasting goodness comforts my soul
When I am down...my spirit lifts when around you
I am found
A positive motivating force within my life
A divine light will forever shine in my heart and mind
Our Heavenly Father blessed our family when
you and Dad
Became husband and wife
Dedicate your time and mind toward
enlightening greatness
Of your family's life
I am so blessed to have you as my Mother
I am so blessed to have you as my #One Fan

I am so blessed to have you as my dear
and trusting friend
I will always love you Mama Sweetie!

(For Dorothy)

Oppositions...Oppositions!!!
4/99

Oppositions...
Been so hurt...for so long
They try to wear you down
Refuse to let it happen
You must remain strong.

You must remain strong, even when
sadness comes, melancholy spirits
Brings a feeling of gloom
With prayer depression is wiped
away all that is too much to consume.

Unknowingly, tears roll down your face
at will...
Refuse to let them stay and spill
So pick up the pieces
Shaking that lonely chill.
Say to yourself, Heavenly Father,
"Peace be still".

Summer's Finale
9/6/98

Summertime is over...a mere perception
Sunshiny day...we stop for fond reflections.

Smile to ourselves as we think of each day's fun
Camps, amusement parks, pools, picnics, reunions,
beaches, vacations
...constantly on the run...oooo lots of fun.

Hopefully in our leisure we read many good books
Realize with future school assignments,
good books help us off-the-hook.

Look around at nature's foliage
Beautiful blossoms still in bloom
Geraniums, coleus, pansies and sunflowers,
various colors...sweet fragrances to consume.

Warm breezes fill the air . . . sunset in the sky
Children go to bed early . . .they ask "why oh why".

The moon is big, round and bright as we kneel
and pray
Thank God so greatly for the many blessings
He has sent us these Sweet Summer Days.

*(Dedicated to "Girls With Hearts" - Bernadette, Jessica,
Rochqual, Nina and Dana)*

By The Grace of God
4/96

Just as the Springtime brings a wonderful
newness to our lives
Let this blessed retirement be the beginning
of your wonderful "rise".

You have most definitely "marched to the beat
of the drummer" always
We know only by the grace of God,
with consistent blessings and praise.

Our precious children need continued nurturing
and guidance
Your easy-going manner and perpetual work gives
your smile glad radiance.

Many more blessings are soon to come to you
with prayer
It is with your strong faith and persistence
we are served with flair.

By The Grace of God.

(Written especially for Gladys C. Whitmyer)

Rejoice!!!!! (It's Good To Ya)
3/29/99

Rejoice, Christ has risen, Alleluia!
Excitement and fun, dressing up on the
run its good to ya.
Yeah, go out of your way each day to be nice and kind
It's a wonderful thing to always help mankind.
Happy Easter to you, with chocolate bunnies,
jelly beans and brightly colored eggs
Decorating your Easter baskets, skipping and
hopping, sometimes on one leg.
It's good to ya, so be generous with hugs,
kisses and pats on the back
Don't forget holding hands, feels good to
all and that is a sweet caring fact.
Let's keep demonstrating love, love we have
for our families and love for our friends
Love we have for nature, love for devotion
until the end.
Make sure you smile with laughter, have a great
good old time
The Easter egg hunt and the Easter egg roll
brings excitement with sunshine.
Its good to ya, keep feeling good as you feel today
Say hello and thank you please, as you go your
merry way!
Rejoice - Christ Has Risen - Alleluia!
*(Dedicated to All of God's Children, Inspired by my mother
Dorothy E. Beverly)*

Come Holy Spirit Keep Teaching Us
5/31/98

We are all spirit filled people
Carriers of the Holy Spirit
Temples of the Spirit of the Lord
Born to be leaders, presenting God's word.

With the Spirit we stand fearless
With the Spirit we stand proud
In the image of the likeness of God
Let us proclaim the mystery of faith out loud.

We are present day apostles
We are people the Spirit has descended upon
Take responsibility to present the word of the Lord
Let the Spirit lead until our day is done.

There's no charge for the gift of the Spirit
Just the will to say yes
An acceptance within our hearts
The beauty of faith and prayer will do the rest.

Let's go back to the basics - Place prayer in our schools
One Love - One God Unity of the Holy Trinity rules.
Knowledge, wisdom, understanding
Fill our hearts with joy and love
Kindle in them deeply the gladness of your love.
"Come Holy Spirit, keep teaching us".
(Dedicated to Father Innocent Njoku)

Thank You For Your Love
5/86

Loving you is easy because you're beautiful...
Everything I do is out of love for you.
I miss you but I'm so happy you gave me enough
to help me be strong
I will never forget the goodness of you.
I will continue to do the things that you admired
about me and always let me know.
I will bring our family and friends together in
unity and love.
Your memory will live forevermore.
May you rest in peace and continue to look after
us in an even greater light.
We love you Dawud and we are doing our best to
understand your cause and your way.
You touched so many hearts and that is a divine
image that so many of us can feel and see.
Thank you for the beautiful children to teach,
guide, love and set free.
Thank you for the wisdom of good nutrition and exercise.
Thank you for the intro to the inspirations of Marley.
Thank you for the example of following your own mind
and living righteously by your own free will.
Thank you for your spiritual emphasis on daily praises
to the Creator, our Almighty God (Jah).
My loving brother Dawud, thank you so graciously for
your love.
(Written at the time of Dawud's death)

WHM-Women's History Month
3/21/97

Ever heard of Women's History Month
That's why we are here today.
To share information and history on some great
women that have passed our way.

One of today's living women that has made a great
difference in our lives
Is Ms. Rosa Parks, when in the back of the bus
she refused to ride.

Dr. Maya Angelou is another great lady
to look up to,
It is living by example, through her poetry
she continues to show me and you.

Singers like Patti LaBelle and Gladys Knight have
entertained audiences for many decades with a
jubilant might.

Self made millionaire, Madame C.J. Walker shows us
that a small hair-care invention can turn into a big
manufacturing business.

Florence Griffith Joyner as glamorous as she may be
Won three gold medals in the 1988 Summer Olympic
Game history.

Many, many women have done big things in our lives
We are taking this month of March for their
accomplishments to be recognized.

I'm A Mere Vessel
9/13/98

Take me dear Lord, body, mind and soul, guide me
Each and everyday where I need and want to be.

Teach me to offer all I do for you
With prayer and love, to thy self be true.

Show me what's right and don't allow me any wrong
Hold me close to your bosom, keeping me healthy
And strong
With You walking beside me, even carrying me
some days
I know everything will be just fine, from your goodness
I'll never stray.

Take me dear Lord, do guide the way
I'm a mere vessel...here to do whatever,
Lord, whatever you say.

I'm a mere vessel Lord, here to do whatever you say.

(written the day my Daddy died)

Tenderhearted Zephyr
8/27/99

I felt a midnight colored, delicate breeze one day
It came and lingered, leaving no room for dismay.

Just as the dark clouds give way to the light,
sheer turmoil will not last
The breeze transpires ever so faintly,
after the storm has passed.

A gentle westward blown, balmy breeze
Capturing all trials and tribulations way up
high above the evergreen trees.

Tender zephyr...wisk away the unsightly cobwebs
Free my mind, with spirit-filled goodness...let it be fed.

Just like a rainbow after the summer's rainfall
you will appear unexpectedly tough and strong....
banishing all tears and fears.
Diligently sweep away all sadness and any despair
Leaving my heart feeling light....free from
burdensome cares.

Holding on...waiting for the storm to pass...a calming
effect...radiantly blue
Tenderhearted zephyr, I await you!

(Dedicated to Kimberly)

Love of Wisdom
12/30/95

Dark wholesome wisdom
African beauty inside and out
A subtle blessing to your family, stepping about
Persistent with your education
Intelligent, strong, independent young lady
Enjoying cultural events, galleries, theaters
and premiers. Bright indigo wisdom
Stepping high and firm out of Essence Magazine
Making everyone proud with each
accomplishment gained
It's no wonder you are knocking at the next degree
Charismatic, unique, bright young lady
A night on the town or cable with your family.
Metallic gold wisdom
Attractive as the north star shining bright
As precious as an amber, with strong willed might
A shining example, ingredients for a role model
Serious, down-to-earth, pleasant young lady
Head to the sky as you walk by.
Blazy red wisdom
Vibrant and fragrant as a rose
Sharing and caring, a delight to your household
Pride for the Deltas
Enthusiastic, brave, witty young lady
Always thrive for success and maintain
the love of wholesome wisdom.
(Dedicated to Marketa LaNean Walker)

Iridescent Jewel
7/19/98

A magnificent rainbow appears across the sky
An iridescent jewel, we wonder how and why.

So infrequently witnessed on this plane
Survival of the fittest, after a beneficial rain.

What a special treat for each eye's encounter
A gorgeous prism enlightens where little else matters.

Too brief what is felt as we experience its
beams of light
"Magnificent" we cry out in sheer wonder...
sheer ecstatic delight.

A blessing, a treasure, a gift, a wondrous treat
Watching in awe, truly knocks us off our feet.

So glorious to see, oh feel the vibrant, variety of colors
Beauty recognized for blessed sisters and brothers.

Phenomenal to catch a glimpse of this miraculous gem
Marvel, wonderment, the holy Spirit is near.

At each rainbow's end, they say there's an
immense pot of gold
Sun shinny skies, yes, blue birds fly for the young
and for the old.

Iridescent jewel, a wondrous, delightful gift above
A blessing from our heavenly Father, truly fills us
with love.

A magnificent rainbow appears across the sky
A multi-colored slate, stretching wide and high.

Beauty profound, fit for the eyes of an African Queen
An iridescent jewel, bold yet serene.

(Dedicated to Angela Owens, NBC4)

Reminiscing on Memories
5/10/96

A decade and it seems like yesterday
"Unbelievable" the cries we all still say
Smiling through our tears
Reminiscing on memories we hold dear
Missing you so very much
It's just you hearty hug and your gentle touch.
Still my dear brother it's a devasting mystery
Wondering what really happen on that
last journey
Knowing that you are with our
Creator above
Feeling comfort with thoughts of your love.
The children are growing up too fast
The babies you left are a thing of the past.
Rest on my sweet brother, my love
Prayer brings a serene heavenly cove
We know you are with your brother Marley
Telling us often not to fret and folly
Reminiscing on memories of you, Dawud
When you taught me to play Bid Wisk
Knowing my next bid would take us to Massachusetts.
Fantastic to see you play our big brother basketball
Without a doubt, you'd give him your all
The only human witnessed full stance on your skull
Knowing the atmosphere would soon
be peaceful and lull
Celebrating your oldest daughter's

High School Graduation
Reminiscing on Memories of you Dawud,
In deed a phenomenal celebration.
(Dedicated to Dayo Aziza Beverly, H.S. Graduation)

Hey There
1-20-05

You with the stars in your eyes
Or is it a mere reflection from mine
A glow, a celestial light
Shines radiant north to south
South to north
To strengthen our weary might
To give purpose
A beginning of sweet sensations
A new revelation
For you for me
To be there for one another
To enhance the quality of life
That only sharing brings.

(For Alben)

Where Have All The Flowers Gone?

Seeds for the flowers have been planted...
Keep them watered and enjoy their blossoms
perpetually.
Our Mothers have a kindness and love for mankind,
especially their children.
Tremendous joy within each family...
Extending from one household to another.
Simplicity is keen...An element bringing happiness
with a precious sheen.
Just being together is all that matters
Hot home-made biscuits with honey and butter.
Going for mile long walks each day,
Picking flowers ecstatically along the way.
Where have all the flowers gone?
With today's automation and constant new
technologies emerging
Be mindful of the exquisite flowers
keep them watered, keep them flourishing.
Where have all the flowers gone?
They are still hanging on...
what are you doing to keep your garden strong?

(Dedicated to Grandmother Maggie A.
Washington-Monroe)

International Love
3/9/99

Across blue waters far across lonely seas
I feel the goodness of your love, the
love you hold deep in your heart for me.

Love that is magnificent, tried, tested, oh so true
So strong, wonderful and kind, I feel no ways blue.

Kindred throughout my being, over the roving years
Wondrous, sweet, kind spirit, depletes all worries
and fears.

Doesn't matter the distance, whether near or far
I feel the presence of your love reflecting in each
twinkling star.

Looking up towards twilight skies...following
a tranquilled full moon
I pray to be safely home, I pray that its
very soon.

Feeling very special, I'm sure its because of your love
International love...a gift cherished from heaven above.
International Love!

(Dedicated to Darrell E. Patterson)

Home Is Where The Heart Feels Good
10/23/98

Home....it's my space, it's my peace, my serenity
It's the warm cozy place God has provided for me.

Home...it's my shelter, my enjoyment,
my haven, my nest
It's where I look forward to a good nights rest.

Home...is where I can fall on my knees
in prayer, in peace
It's where I can come inside and on life get a
renewed lease.

Home...is where I can decorate till
my hearts content
It's where my body, mind and soul
absorbs what's
heaven sent.

Home...is where I can sit and meditate for hours
It's where I can prune my plants and marvel
the varied colored flowers.

Home...is where I read and write with a hearty might
It's where I plan to do what I know is right.

Home...is where we invite family
and friends for fellowship

It's where we play parlor games, play music,
dance and laugh at that and this.

Home is where the heart feels good!

(Another poem for Maya)

Bring Back The Holy Spirit
3-9-99

Bring back the Holy Spirit,
planted deep, deep in our souls
Unite in righteous blessings
keeping us miraculously whole.

Strong beings of mother earth
bountifully given
Encourage spirituality an enlightening
way of living.

With the Holy Spirit we are one
With the Holy Spirit we are filled
Bring back the Holy Spirit, we
know its God's will.

(Dedicated to Fr. Innocent)

Your Face
5/22/96

I love your face
I love the way you smile at me
I love the grace
The grace and love God has given
you and me.

The fragrance of the rose
Fills our hearts with beauty chose
So sweet and wonderful
I love your face.

Don't ever leave me my strong knight
I love you more each day with a stronger might
I love your face.

So golden firm and smooth
It's tantalizing the way you move
Moving always in the right direction
Your easy manner projects little or no friction
I love, love your face.

Our Passion
11/22/97

Never trade our passion for distance Sweetheart
Let fire and love tenderly embrace us, warm our hearts.

Roses and lilies fragrantly blanket our lives
Sweet as honey, strong as a million bee hives.

Comfort and understanding come at us two-fold
Radiance and smiles sparkle gently...light our souls.

Tinkling bells and violins soar
Ecstasy strongly heightens our being forevermore.

Share...care, unity sharply prevails
Smooth, keen and serene as any ships' sails.

Prayer and faith, key elements encouraging our hearts
Blessings and splendor righteousness and truth
we can not impart.

Never trade our passion for distance My Love
It has the grandeur and power of sweet Heaven above.

Inside Out
11/21/02

Nights...long cold and bleak
Leave me all alone with no one
To hold...no one to hold me
Oh set me free...free from
Lopped-sided bonds, deceit and
Disrespect
Let me once again feel goodness
Goodness of sharing infinitely.
Love and being loved.
Betcha-by-golly-wow...
True love never dies
True love, a many splendid thing.
Smile into each others' smiles
Tender touch with only our eyes
Surrender to ultimate satisfaction
Our sole being...fall into oblivion
Turn cold bleakness inside out.

Love's Surrender
1/20/05

Talk love...Dream love
Surround self by love
Perpetual goodness...sweet love
Love's atmosphere
Embodied...bound...surrounded by love
Love of siblings
Support Share Ideas and Life
Speak truths - Sweet togetherness
Just knowing you are close by
Somewhere near
Tender delight of Mother's devoted love
Sacrifice since existence
Unconditional...just because
Implicit love of nature
A mirage...a mystical horizon
Diamonds scattered across blanket of
Tranquilled blue
Fragrant wild flowers...cascade of beauty
Along highways...across emerald meadows
Love of man for woman...woman for man
Guide Protect Support each other
Sweet love I surrender!

(For Haki)

Mesmerized Baby to Ecstasy
10/20/01

Mesmerized Baby to ecstasy
This love for you will forever be
Decades of love Darling and pure Fantasy.
Fine like vintage wine and antique lace
Oh so...luscious to me.
Ooooo...I'm still feeling you Baby
Even...when your presence I can not see.
Melodic, Sensational. Enchanting...
A sheer delight...heighten by anticipated
Desires of your enduring might.
Mesmerized Baby to ecstasy
This love for you will forever be.
Ooooo...Baby Sweet Darling you're any angel
My Sugar, Honey, Cup of Tea.
Stay with me Baby...I'm here for you...won't
You be here for me?
Mesmerized Baby to ecstasy
This love for you will forever be.
Said we'd always have each others back
Noooo Baby, now we can't do that
Hanging out across the track and that's
truly a fact.
Ooooo Baby Sweet Darling...gonna tighten up
Our thing
Gonna let it simmer to sweet vibrations.
Gonna, don't you wanna hear twinkling bells ring?
I'm mesmerized Baby to ecstasy

Mesmerized by your love for me.
Perpetual love in my heart Sweet Darling
Will forever be
Can't you see...Don't have to shop around
Anymore, yes stay right here Baby
I have all the love you need
Cause I'm mesmerized Baby to Ecstasy!
Mesmerized by your love for me.

(Dedicated to Smokey Robinson)

My Heart Speaks
2/15/02

The voice within my heart speaks
Of true love
The bond between us two.
Talk...whisper...unity of power
Enhance our present and future desires.
Keep us healthy, happy and strong
When all else fails...love and unity
Says nothing is really wrong.
Brings a million tons of power
Hour by hour...day by day
Prayer is recipient of God's holy
Blessings
Miraculous graces shows the way.
The voice within my heart
Tells me what to do...where to go
It's all I know.
It's good...It's on
It's a treasure born
It's all that shows
It's the only way to go
It tells me you really do love me
And oh how I love you so.
Listening to the voice within my heart
Speak...keeps me loving unconditionally.

A New Love Thang
11/4/03

Butterflies, Butterflies
You are reason why
Flit around flower to flower
I feel you most during midnight hour
Bold light strong at the same time
Colorful vibrant vividly sweet
All around marvelous light shines
Birds sing tweet tweet.

Butterflies, Butterflies
Won't you ease some today
Just a bit ...you don't have to go away
I love the youthful yummy feeling and
Happiness you forever bring
Keep my heart happy...make my love sing.

Butterflies, Butterflies
You keep doing your thing
I love the way your melody rings
I actually don't mind...
If you stay around awhile
If you do...it will help keep our
love thang brand new.

Girlfriend
5/04/02

Girlfriend Girlfriend!

I am coming up the rough side of the
mountain with You.
Oh so ecstatic to have this poetry thing
Camouflages all that is blah and blue.

Share deeply spoken words from our devoted hearts
Energized by glow of your wonderful spirit
Every since we met...from the very start.

Girlfriend Girlfriend!

Enjoy each presentation with dramatic expressions
Oh so deep from within
Extend a unique, genuine talent...perpetually giving
an extra twist or spin.

Only by the grace of God can we begin to create
Keep prayer and love best friends
Our destiny...Our fate.

Girlfriend Girlfriend!

Stand on peaked mountain tops...your smiling
Faces to indigo skies

Perpetually reaching back to bring another
on High.

Miraculously...receive from varied inspiration
All encouragement you have consistently given.
Invigorate graces...choose an immaculate
Way of living.

Girlfriend Girlfriend!

Never stop moving and grooving...reading and writing
Girlfriend
Documenting our courageous heritage and real
true history
it's all we will have in the end...Girlfriend!

*(Dedicated to my poetic Girlfriends, Lottie Mae
McDonald "GrandMa Slam", Billye O'Kera J. Joy Alford,
a.k.a. Sistah Joy, C. Carolyn Joyner, Angela Boykin-
Turnbull, Abena Disroe, C. Jeanean Gibbs, Linda Beverly,
Kisha Morris, Doris Thomas, Alisha McGraw, Mercedes
Vessels, Ambrosia Shepherd, Forestine Bynum, "Black
Beauty" and last but not least my precious "Girls With
Hearts" Bernadette Brown, Jessica Gaines, Nina Makel,
Dana Makel and Rochqual Cain)*

Complications!!
2/8/03

I heard Maya say the other day
"We are more a like than different".
So why in the world would anyone
Feel superiority would bring contentment?
The world has a way of making everyone feel
Like a blade of grass...
You can not just cut us back with a lawn mower
Quick and ever so fast.
We are strong sturdy trees with roots embedded
Deeply towards equality and justice
Stand up for our rights, deal steadfast
Do away with prejudice and injustice.
We stand tall, we stand erect
We stand to make a difference in the world
Insist on doing the right thing
Towards every woman, man, boy and girl.
Complications, consistently on the rise
Even as we recognize our freedom
As an ongoing struggle today
We must take action, find a solution
In our lives to alleviate stress and dismay.
Let us unite...stand up for what is right
Never to give up the fight...through God's
Holy light
We are energized with a strong will and might.
Let us be like that tree planted by the water
Handle all adversities and complications

Meticulously, patiently and peacefully
Without falter..

*(Dedicated in Memory of My Beloved Sister, My Friend,
My Confidant Bernadette Marita Beverly-Shafer)*

A Poem Looking 4 A Title
1/30/03

Through poetry, our voices are heard
Heart to heart talks
Designed by the spoken word.

Through poetry, we paint phenomenal, pretty Pictures
Expressions from our hearts, whether reality Or fiction.

Through poetry, we unite in a bond of strength
and action
Smiling all the while to get another's reaction.

Through poetry our lives have sensational splendor
Like radiant rainbows rising...bursting through
Clouds of thunder.

Through poetry we always have something to do
Whether reading or writing, let it be good to you.

Through poetry we pour out the love of
our hearts Soul
Feeling oh so yummy, when in your arms, your love
You hold.

Through poetry we take a stand for
what is richly Righteous
Teaching our children to be strong, spiritual,
Intelligent, caring and courageous.

Through poetry we share most intimate truths
Appreciating the positive energies, always under roof.

All of this through poetry????

It is no wonder poetry is my passion!

(Dedicated to Kwame Alexander)

I'll Always Be Daddy's Girl
5/28/03

I want to dance with my Daddy again too
I want to be his little girl so happy, so true.
I want to whisper secrets and watch Daddy smile
I want to hear him say "too bad they can't stay
small a longer while".
I'll Always Be Daddy's Girl.
I want to wake in the mornings to his melodic
Mellow songs
I want to feel safe, warm and strong as Daddy holds
Me in his arms.
I want to listen to his wit and wisdom all night
I want to have Daddy hug me and say, everything
Is going to be alright.
I'll Always Be Daddy's Girl.
I want to hear him say "is everybody happy"
then send me on a chore, saying "you not back yet,
Girl, make it snappy".
I want to turn back the hands of time
And in my daily life feel Daddy's love shine.
I'll always be Daddy's girl!

(For the Late Daniel L. Beverly, Sr., Father's Day 2003)

A Poem for Gil Scott-Heron
7/4/99

You are for real that is what I like about you so
Telling it just like it is wherever you go.

Knowing people don't always want to
hear the truth
Gil you've been giving it to us loud and strong,
since our youth.

My Daddy loved all six of his girls,
thought it was the only way to be
"Daddy Loves His Girl", a phenomenal
favorite, so wondrously from you to me.

You told us "The Revolution Will Not Be
Televised" and all about "Watergate Blues"
Left us quite enlightened about "Whitey on the
Moon", why oh why the necessity,
we don't have any clues.

Wise beyond your years,
insight shared with many,
With each performance,
you carry a cornucopia of plenty.

Thank you Holy Spirit for bringing Gil to
Federal City College
Thank you Brother Gil

for an abundance of goodness,
perpetually sharing creative knowledge.

(Dedicated to Gil Scott-Heron after his performance at "Blues Alley", Georgetown, D.C., Midnight, July 3, 1999)

Sunflower in Sunshine
7/3/99

Sunflower standing out among
the flowers in the garden
Oh so tall and strong in the Sunshine
With sweet, sweet admiration
echoes of nature's chisel-carved
spirit surrounds what's truly thine.

Watching over a variety of others
Your strength encourages artistic
creativity in many sisters
and brothers.

Decade after decade your wisdom
and wit flourish the earth
Enlightening, fulfilling, giving
Praises with promise and blessings
Of the spoken word, with each new birth.

Oh...I feel your presence ever so
greatly Sunflower
Artistically creating
Through fiery, piercing heat,
Year by year, day-by-day,
Hour by hour.

Melodic words of power, politics, war
and corruption

Mixed with love, peace and blessings
Adoringly moving towards perfection.

Sunflower, Sunflower highly influential
standing out uniquely among the rest
Sunflower in sunshine...developing a
"Midas" sheen, you are among greats
You are the best.

(Another poem for Gil Scott-Heron)

It's Up To Me
11/23/02

Be a leader
Even if it means standing alone
Be unique
Have a style and mind of your own.
Be steadfast, solid on your convictions
Stand up for your predictions
Initiate brand new traditions
Be truthful, especially to self
Know honesty and love wins above all else.
Be on time
Be the first in line
You just might get a quarter instead of a dime.
Be thankful and prayerful morning noon and night
God our Father will lead you
Guide you towards what is right.
Be pleasant, be optimistic, smile say hello first
Yes, thank you, please, make them daily verse.
Be wise and witty - success will be for thee
All the while saying "if it is to be,
It's up to me".

(Dedicated to Korin)

Committed
4/9/05 (Haiku # 56)

As we travel loves'
Road...around each corner I
Will be there 4U!

About the Author

Sylvia Dianne Beverly is a native of Washington, D.C. She is the oldest girl of nine children and attributes her exceptional leadership abilities to this fact. Her mother is her best friend and #One Fan. Ms. Beverly attended the University of the District of Columbia, majoring in English and studying under internationally acknowledged writer and poet, Gil Scott-Heron. Ms. Beverly frequently shares original poetry and poetry of Dr. Maya Angelou. She has presented poetry around the Washington Metropolitan Area, in other states and at the Lewisham Theater in Brixton, London, England. Ms. Beverly recently retired from federal government service of 35 years and is enjoying the freedom of reading, writing and presenting poetry. She is known as "Ladi Di" and affectionately called "Love Poet". A blessing for her, she has presented at many schools, libraries, museums, galleries, theaters and churches. Celebrating National Poetry Month 2004, she performed on WHUT "Evening Exchange" with Kojo Namdi. You may catch a glimpse of "Ladi Di" on CTV76, promoting poetry in Prince George County and the Nation's Capitol. Ms. Beverly is the founder/director of "Girls and Boys with Hearts" Youth Poetry Group and is a founding member of "Collective Voices", sisterhood of poets.

Ms. Beverly is a proud member of "Poets in Progress", under the direction of Poet Laureate of the District of Columbia, Dolores Kendrick. Giving back to the community, Ms. Beverly shares poetry with residence at Med-Link Nursing Facility, Marwood Seniors Apts., and is a volunteer for Black Women In Sisterhood for Action (BISA) where she is also, their "Poet In Residence". Recognizing Black History February 2005, she hosts the 5th Annual Black History Poetry Festival at Iverson Mall, Hillcrest Heights, Md. She is available to help celebrate your next event with your church, family or organization. Ms. Beverly resides in Prince Georges County, Maryland.

Contact Ladi Di syladydi@comcast.net

Printed and bound by PG in the USA